Aether

by Emma Howlett

Aether was first performed at Summerhall, Edinburgh Fringe on 31 July 2025. It transferred to the Jermyn Street Theatre, London, on 16 March 2026.

Aether
by Emma Howlett

CAST

ONE	Sophie Kean
TWO	Abby McCann
THREE	Anna Marks Pryce
FOUR	Gemma Barnett

CREATIVES

Writer and Director	Emma Howlett
Set and Costume Designer	Ellie Wintour
Lighting Designer	Ed Saunders
Composer and Sound Designer	Sarah Spencer
Dramaturg	Sophie Kean

CAST

SOPHIE KEAN | ONE

Theatre includes: *My Master Builder* (Wyndham's Theatre); *Her Green Hell* (Theatre Royal Bath/Theatre Royal Plymouth/Summerhall/VAULT Festival); *Scenes for John* (National Theatre Studio); *Sisters Three* (Summerhall).

Sophie trained at Rose Bruford College and studied at the University of Cambridge.

ABBY MCCANN | TWO

Theatre includes: *Sisters Three* (Summerhall); *Looking For Giants* (Kings Head/Underbelly); *Ordinary Sex* (in development).

Short film includes: *Laura and Sophia* (dir. Michael Jobling); *Can't A Girl?* (dir. Isabel Ion); *Larking* (Dir. Selwin Hulme Teague).

Abby studied at the University of Oxford where she won the Juliet Bernard Memorial Prize as Most Promising Actress.

ANNA MARKS PRYCE | THREE

Theatre includes: *Rapunzel: A Hairy Tale* (Tobacco Factory Theatres); *Myrninerest: The Inside/Outside Life of Madge Gill* (Art in the Docks); *It's ok, I still think you're great* (Barons Court Theatre); *4 girls the first letter e* (Kings Head Theatre); *The Creature: Frankenstein Retold* (Rose Theatre, Kingston/Oldenburgisches Staatstheater).

Voiceover includes: *Alma Mater* (Almeida Theatre)

Anna trained at Mountview.

GEMMA BARNETT | FOUR

Theatre includes: *REVENGE: After the Levoyah* (Soho Theatre / Yard Theatre); *The Invincibles* (Queens Theatre, Hornchurch); *The Beach House* (Park Theatre); *Crimea 5am* (Kiln Theatre); *Agatha* (Pleasance Theatre); *Dr Korczak's Example* (Leeds Playhouse); *A Hundred Words for Snow* (Trafalgar Studios/Winner of Offie Best Solo Performer); *A Midsummer Night's Dream* (Shakespeare in the Squares).

TV includes: *Casualty* (BBC).

Short film includes: *Please Carry On* (BFI Flare); *Bridge* (BBC & Kusini Productions); *Preggo* (Fidge Films); *Miss* (Mad Girl Productions).

Gemma trained at Oxford School of Drama.

CREATIVES

EMMA HOWLETT | WRITER AND DIRECTOR

Emma Howlett is a British-Irish theatre director and writer from Bath, now based in London, staging new work and reinventing classics across the UK and in Europe. She is Artistic Director of theatregoose, for which she writes, directs and produces an expanding repertoire of critically acclaimed work. *Aether* is the company's third show.

In 2025, she was named one of The Stage's Fringe Five for *Aether* and her work at theatregoose, and won the inaugural Hugo Burge Foundation New Theatre Writing Residency, the first Summerhall Arts' Creative Residency, and the John Fernald Directing Award from the Equity Charitable Trust.

Theatre as Writer-Director includes: *Sisters Three* (Summerhall); *Her Green Hell* (Theatre Royal Bath/Theatre Royal Plymouth/Summerhall/VAULT Festival).

Theatre as Director includes: *Grounded* (Bridge Theatre Brussels); *Copenhagen* dir. after Polly Findlay (Theatre Royal Bath/UK Tour); *Enron* (Oxford Playhouse).

ELLIE WINTOUR | SET AND COSTUME DESIGNER

Theatre as Designer include: *Breaking Bach* (Edinburgh International Festival), *Miles* (Southwark Playhouse); *855-FOR-TRUTH* (The Bridge Theatre, Brussels); *Thanks for Having Me* (Riverside Studios); *Dead Dad Death Cult* (Battersea Arts Centre); *Florence* (Pleasance/The Other Palace); *Chef* (The Gaiety Theatre/Scottish Tour); *Blizzard* (Soho Theatre); *Grounded* (Bridge Theatre, Brussels).

Concerts as Co-Creative Director includes: *Porridge Radio at the Pompidou Centre* (Centre Pompidou, Paris) and albums Waterslide, Diving Board, Ladder to the Sky and Every Bad.

Theatre as an Associate Designer to Es Devlin include: Dua Lipa's *Future Nostalgia World Tour*; promenade dance piece *Salamander* (Brisbane Festival); *The Crucible* (The National Theatre/Gielgud Theatre), *Here Not*

Here (Gothenburg Opera House), *An Atlas of Es Devlin* (The Cooper Hewitt Museum) and Beyoncé's *Renaissance World Tour*.

ED SAUNDERS | LIGHTING DESIGNER

Theatre as Lighting Designer includes: *Her Green Hell* (Theatre Royal Plymouth/Theatre Royal Bath/Summerhall/VAULT Festival); *Sisters Three* (Summerhall); *Bitter Lemons* and *Cold Water* (Park Theatre); *Grounded* (Bridge Theatre Brussels).

Dance as Lighting Designer includes: *Breaking Bach* (Edinburgh Festival Theatre); *The Joystick and The Reins* (Bold Tendencies/Actoral, Marseille/ Dansehallerne, Copenhagen); *COWPUNCHER MY ASS* (Royal Festival Hall, Southbank Centre); *Eye to Eye* (Institute of Contemporary Arts); *DN2* and *No Land B* (The Place/Tour).

Dance as Co-Lighting Designer and Programmer: *BORNSICK* (Serpentine/ Edinburgh Arts Festival).

Music as Lighting Designer includes: *San Remo* (Glastonbury Festival); *Porridge Radio at the Pompidou Centre* (Centre Pompidou, Paris); *The Seed, The Sinkhole, The Flower and the Flare* (Institute of Contemporary Arts); *Rising Presents Chisara Agor* and *An Evening in Nocturnal Sun* (Roundhouse Studio Theatre).

Fashion as Lighting Designer includes: *Pressiat* (Paris); *Lueder* (London); *British Fashion Council NEWGEN* (180 The Strand).

Opera as Lighting Designer includes: *A Midsummer Night's Dream* (Opera Holland Park).

SARAH SPENCER | COMPOSER AND SOUND DESIGNER

Theatre as Composer & Sound Designer include: *1.17am, or until the words run out* (Finborough Theatre); *Storms, Maybe Snow* (Seven Dials Playhouse/Union Theatre/Drayton Arms Theatre/Cockpit Theatre); *Lysistrata, The Lodger, Pygmalion, Doctor Faustus* (Old Red Lion Theatre); *Foolish* (The Courtyard Theatre); *Scatter* (Underbelly Edinburgh/ Underbelly Boulevard Soho); *Florence* (The Other Palace/Greenside Edinburgh); *Mumsplaining* (Canal Café Theatre); *How To Kill a Chicken* (The Actors Theatre, Brighton); *Looking for Giants* (Underbell/King's Head Theatre); *Yes, We're Related* (The Other Palace; Underbelly Edinburgh); *Tending* (Brixton House/Bush Theatre/Riverside Studios/Theatre Royal Bath); *Sisters Three* (Summerhall); *Grounded* (Bridge Theatre, Brussels); *Her Green Hell* (Theatre Royal Bath/Theatre Royal Plymouth/Summerhall, VAULT Festival); *Move Fast and Break Things* (Summerhall); *Pepi and*

Me (Camden People's Theatre); *Funk Me Up* (Tipsy Bear Berlin); *FEVER!* (Miami); *How To Save a Rock* (Pleasance/UK Tour/Theatre by the Lake).

Theatre as Sound Designer include: *Pear Phobia* (Soho Theatre/Underbelly Edinburgh/Underbelly Boulevard Soho); *Late With Pear* (Underbelly Edinburgh); *The Great Gatsby* (European Tour); *KAREN* (Omnibus Theatre; The Other Palace; Seven Dials Playhouse; Underbelly Boulevard Soho).

Theatre as Composer, Pianist & Performer include: *Project Dictator* (UK & Norway Tour); *The Tournament* (Matchstick Piehouse).

Film and TV as Composer includes: *The Trees* (Tilda Swinton/Eye Film Museum Amsterdam); *Good Night Stories For Rebel Girls* (Makematic).

Film as Assistant Composer: *Tunnelen* (International Cinematic Release).

theatregoose.

theatregoose is the work of writer-director Emma Howlett with designers Ellie Wintour, Ed Saunders, Sarah Spencer, dramaturg and performer Sophie Kean, and a growing ensemble of actors.

After establishing the company at the University of Oxford for her early directorial work in 2018, Howlett launched theatregoose professionally with debut show *Her Green Hell* (VAULT Festival/Summerhall/Theatre Royal Plymouth/Theatre Royal Bath) in 2023, followed by *Sisters Three* (Summerhall) in 2024. The company's third show, *Aether* (Summerhall/Jermyn Street Theatre), debuted in 2025 and transfers in 2026. Their fourth show will debut at Summerhall in 2026.

JERMYN STREET THEATRE

The West End's Studio Theatre

Jermyn Street Theatre is the West End's Studio Theatre, a home for extraordinary artists and curious audiences for over thirty years. Led by Artistic Director **Stella Powell-Jones**, Executive Director **Penny Horner**, and Co-Artistic Director and Executive Producer **David Doyle**, Jermyn Street Theatre stages superb classics and thrilling new plays with theatrical legends alongside those taking their first steps in the industry.

In 1994, Co-Founders Penny Horner and Howard Jameson came down the stairs of 16b Jermyn Street for the first time and saw what could be: a studio theatre right in the centre of town where theatre artists could afford to take risks, and where audiences could afford to see the work. The theatre upholds those commitments today, and in the three decades since has created ambitious work that has won countless awards and reached global audiences through transfers across the UK, Broadway, and beyond. In 2017, the theatre became a full-time producing house. In 2021, it made history as the first to win The Stage Award for Fringe Theatre of the Year for a second time. In 2024, the theatre celebrated its thirtieth anniversary with productions including the world premieres of **Roy Williams**' OffWestEnd award-winning adaptation of **Sam Selvon**'s *The Lonely Londoners* and the West End transfer of **Katherine Moar**'s debut play *Farm Hall*.

↑ Gamba Cole, Romario Simpson, Tobi Bakare in *The Lonely Londoners* at Jermyn Street Theatre, photo by Alex Brenner

JERMYN STREET THEATRE

Honorary Patron
HRH Princess Michael of Kent

Patrons
Lord Julian Kitchener-Fellowes
Lady Emma Kitchener-Fellowes

Sir Michael Gambon was our treasured Patron until his death in 2023.

Board of Trustees
Penny Horner
Howard Jameson (Chair)
Chris Parkinson
Vikram Sivalingam
Steve Norris

Artistic Director
Stella Powell-Jones

Executive Director
Penny Horner

Co-Artistic Director & Executive Producer
David Doyle

Carne Deputy Director*
Al Miller
Kwame Owusu

Producer
Jessie Anand

Production Manager
Lucy Mewis-McKerrow

Marketing Manager
Natasha Ketel

Graphic Designer
Ciaran Walsh

PR
KMPR

Associate Artists
Darren Sinnott
Ebenezer Bamgboye

Associate Designer
Louie Whitemore

Business Development
Chris Parkinson

Box Office Manager
Alex Pearson

Day Box Office Team
Amanda Grace**
Pippa Lee

Duty Managers
Ellie Burbeary
Christina Gazelidis
Adam Lilley
Mark Magill

Bar Team
Mandy Berger
Lydia Boffey
Sukiana Hashamy
Aren Johnston
Pippa Lee

Web Design
Robin Powell / Ideasfor

Web Development
Robert Iles / Dynamic Listing

Jermyn Street Theatre staff salaries are supported by

BackstageTrust

Core costs are supported by Marit Mohn DBE and Robert Westlake.

* *The Carne Deputy Director position is supported by Philip Carne MBE and Christine Carne.*

** *Membership Manager*

Jermyn Street Theatre is a Registered Charity
No. 1186940

Our Friends

Director's Circle

Anonymous
Philip Carne MBE &
  Christine Carne
Jocelyn Abbey &
  Tom Carney
Colin Clark RIP
Lynette & Robert Craig
Carol and Gary Fethke
Flora Fraser
Robert & Pirjo Gardiner
Ros & Duncan McMillan
Leslie &
  Peter MacLeod-Miller
Marit Mohn DBE &
  Robert Westlake
Marjorie Simonds-
  Gooding
Peter Soros &
  Electra Toub
Melanie Vere Nicoll

Miranda Friends

Anonymous
Anthony Ashplant
Gyles &
  Michèle Brandreth
Sylvia de Bertodano
Anthony Cardew
Robyn Durie
Richard Edgecliffe-
  Johnson
Nora Franglen
Mary Godwin
Ros & Alan Haigh
Diana Houghton
Phyllis Huvos
John Hyatt
Christopher Imrie
Mark Jones
Pauline Kelly
Marta Kinally
Hilary King
Yvonne Koenig
Christine MacCallum
Keith MacDonald
Jane Mennie
Tiziana Morosetti
Charles Paine
Alexander Powell
Iain Reid
Ros Shelley
Jenny Sheridan
Brian Smith
Frank Southern
Mark Tantam
Paul Taylor
Geraldine Terry
Sandra Treagus
Brian & Esme Tyers
John Wise

Ariel Friends

Richard &
  Daisy Alexander
Derek Baum
Stephen Baxter
Philip Bent
Martin Blackburn
Dmitry Bosky
Katie Bradford
Nigel Britten
Donald Campbell
James Carroll
Ted Craig
Jeanette Culver
John Dale
Shomit Dutta
Jill & Paul Dymock
Aidan & Kate Elliott
Bernard Fleckney
James Friedenthal
Anthony Gabriel
Roger Gaynham
Paul Guinery
Diana Halfnight
Eleanor Harvey
Andrew Hughes
Jennifer Jacobs
David Lanch
Caroline Latham
George Mackay
Keith MacDonald
Vivien Macmillan-Smith
Ernest Meikle
Sir Aaron Mowla
Nicky Oliver
Kate & John Peck
Lydia Petty
Adrian Platt
Margaret Ramage
Carolyn Shapiro
Carol Shephard-Blandy
Nigel Silby
Sir Bernard Silverman
Jeremy Simons
Jenny Skilbeck
Philip Somervail
Keith Steadman
Jan Topman
Gary Trimby
George Warren
Lavinia Webb
Jeremy &
  Kim White Foundation

AETHER

Emma Howlett

Characters

ONE / SOPHIE
TWO / FLORENCE / KATIE
THREE / ADELAIDE
FOUR / HYPATIA

Other Characters of the Aether-verse

STEVEN WEINBERG
GIRLFRIEND
SUPERVISOR
PHYSICIST 1
PHYSICIST 2
STUDENT 1
STUDENT 2
STUDENT 3
LIBRARIAN
GENTLEMAN 1
GENTLEMAN 2
GENTLEMAN 3
WILLIAM CROOKES
ARTHUR CONAN DOYLE
HARRY HOUDINI
LEO HERRMANN
FIRING SQUAD 1
FIRING SQUAD 2
JOURNALIST 1
JOURNALIST 2
JOURNALIST 3

Setting

A portion of visible, blue, ordinary matter that becomes:

A theatre.

A spirit cabinet.

A lecture hall.

A telescope.

A high-energy particle accelerator.

+

A blue velvet curtain, obscuring the vastness of the unobservable universe.

Notes on Performance

Where a specific city is mentioned, change to the city of performance.

Rules of the Show / the Universe

(1) What you see is not always what you get.

(2) Everything you think you know, you do not.

(3) Some things are not meant to be understood.

(4) Nature does not care what we believe or what we think is beautiful, *it just is*.

This text went to press before the end of rehearsals and so may differ slightly from the play as performed.

PROLOGUE

The blue, observable universe is bare but for a microphone on a stand and a small circular podium, that turns, almost imperceptibly, at all times.

We hear a few testing thuds on the mic.

The clearing of throats.

Voices.

ONE	Please don't be alarmed. Disembodied voices tend to alarm, we've found.
	But don't assume that because you can't see us, we are any less real.
	Impossibly, the microphone stand moves.
	See?
TWO	We are here, gathered around this microphone, leaning in to speak to you for the first time in *your* history.
THREE	We've been playing a sort of hide and seek with you for a few millennia now. And to be frank, it's been quite a boring game for us so far. Only very recently have you been putting in

	any effort at all.
FOUR	So we'd like to propose a truce. Temporarily, of course.
ONE	Because you seem to be losing heart already.
TWO	And we'd hate for the game to end.
THREE	So we're going to tell you a story. Or five. Stories of your own. That might, proverbially, shed some light.
TWO	To help you make a leap.
THREE	Of imagination.
ONE	Of faith.
FOUR	Of whatever you like.
TWO	Into the dark.
THREE	But before we *optically* join you on the other side.
FOUR	Let's all *conceptually* get on the same page.
ONE	It's important you know that what you are looking at is only

	five percent of what is actually in front of you.
THREE	That the blue matter in this room represents what you *know* is in the universe, and that everything else, the rest of the city of London, represents the majority that you do not.
FOUR	*You* are part of the blue. *We* are part of the rest.
ONE	You are the smudge and we are the window.
THREE	You are the fly and we are the buffalo.
FOUR	If the buffalo was *invisible* to the fly.

TWO	We're going to let you sit with that thought for a moment.
	.
FOUR	And now you've had ample time to consider the thrilling enormity of your ignorance.
ONE	The infinite opportunities for discovery that await.
THREE	We can begin.

A kick of music as four PARTICLES *reveal themselves.*

The PARTICLES *dance through a quantum realm to find themselves in the game-show world of:*

Wheel of Fortune [Standard Model Edition]

A spinning wheel with the particles of the Standard Model.

If it was going to be literal (<u>which it shouldn't be</u>) it would look something like this:

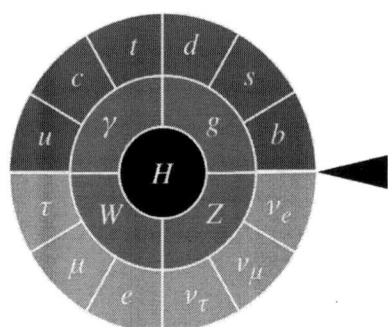

The PARTICLES *introduce the game show in general American accents.*

ONE
Look
at all those
fabulous particles
up for grabs, tonight
people.

TWO
Including,
for those who seek
the fast lane in life,
the sparkling
photon,
your ticket to commuting
at the speed of light,
ladies and gentlemen.

Crowd laugh track.

THREE
No matter what
mood you're in,
enjoy the ride of life as an
electron,
the household name
of the Standard Model,
with a unique 'spin'
that'll make you
a magnetic social force.

FOUR
Or if you prefer
ultimate power,
our newest addition
to the wheel,
the Higgs Boson,
humbly called
the 'God' particle,
is for the lovable
control freaks amongst you.

ONE
Endless
possibilities to be won.

	All of the known particles and three of the four known forces.
TWO	Gravity's not on the cards, people, we're sorry. It doesn't fit the model!
THREE	Neither does anti-matter, for that *matter,*
	Crowd laugh track.
	so we're just going to pretend it doesn't exist!!!!!!
FOUR	Aaaaaand here's your host, Nobel Prize Winner for Physics and my personal favourite non-fiction writer to quote at a dinner party: the man who named it the Standard Model in the first place:
	It's Steeeeeeeven Weinberg!
	Applause track as ONE *takes the microphone and becomes* STEVEN WEINBERG.
STEVEN	Good evening. I'm a slightly upbeat version of Steven Weinberg. I'm honoured to be here with you tonight. It's a beautiful evening to convert some energy.

                        So!
                        Who is our first
                        contestant?

                        TWO on the podium with the Southern Belle accent of a pageant queen.

TWO   Honoured
                        to be here.
                        I'm afraid I can't
                        give you my name
                        because humanity hasn't
                        found or given me one yet.

STEVEN   Little Miss Mysterious!
                        I hear you were born
                        early on in the universe,
                        is that correct?
                        (But I won't ask a lady
                        her age.)

TWO   I'll forgive you that faux pas, Steven.
                        Yes. I admit, I was born
                        very shortly after the
                        Big
                        Bang.
                        It was a lively time to grow up.

STEVEN   Well, you don't look a day over
                        one billion!

TWO   You flatter me.

STEVEN   And where is it you call
                        home?

TWO   My whole life,
                        I lived in a clump of my kind
                        that surrounded the
                        Milky Way.
                        Never left.

                        Occupationally,
                        I formed the galaxy itself,

	but I retired a few billion years ago. I figured no need for heavy lifting in my later years.
	STEVEN *holds a finger to his ear.*
STEVEN	My producers tell me you've never interacted with light before. Can that be true?
TWO	Yes. I'm a little shy.
	Crowd laugh track.
STEVEN	Well, tonight you get to start a new life in the observable universe. How do you feel?
TWO	So excited to be finally seen for who I really am.
STEVEN	Then let's have a spin of the wheel!
	TWO *spins the wheel.*
	Clickclickclickclickclickclick-click-click-click—click—click————click.
	The arrow hypothetically lands on 's'.
	The Strange Quark.
	Applause track.

	Congratulations, Weirdo! You will start life as a Strange Quark!
TWO	What's so strange about it?
STEVEN	Nothing! That's a physicist's idea of a joke. Just another beautiful building block of the universe, darlin'. That's the game. Who's next?

THREE *spins. It would land on 'c'. Charm Quark.*

A smooth criminal
has entered the building!
Enjoy your prize,
life as a
Charm Quark
awaits!

Don't go breaking
too many hearts.

FOUR *spins. It would land on 't'. Truth/ Top Quark.*

We'll take your word for it!
A Truth Quark
among us!

TWO *takes over as* STEVEN. ONE *spins.*

Last but not least…

'b'. Beauty/Bottom Quark.

Ladies and gentlemen,
feast your eyes,
we have a

PROLOGUE   13

Beauty Quark!
What a win.

STEVEN *holds the mic to* ONE*'s mouth.*

ONE

I'd like to thank my

Mom –

STEVEN *cuts her off.*

STEVEN

It's been a
great game tonight,
but your lives are
just beginning.
You know your
calling.
It's time to get to
work.
If you'd be so kind
as to
please

The world slows down.

assume

the
position.

The four PARTICLES *take starting
positions, as if at the beginning of a race.*

Suddenly, we are in a quantum realm.

A techno beat builds.

In slow motion, the PARTICLES *sprint
towards one another.*

As they collide, a blinding light reveals...

◯

THE STUDENT
CAMBRIDGE. 2026 AD.

...SOPHIE, *a PhD candidate at the University of Cambridge, at the podium.*

The other PARTICLES *rebound.*

THREE	Sophie is three years into her PhD in particle physics.
TWO	Sophie works on an experiment in Geneva that sends thousands of measurements to her computer every day.
FOUR	Sophie stares at a screen, analysing data she hopes will reveal something no-one has ever known.
THREE	Sophie's team is one of many racing to find the answer

	to humanity's greatest unsolved mystery.
TWO	The case of the universe's missing matter.
THREE	But so far, in the forty-five years since the search began, no-one has found a thing.
FOUR	Not.
TWO	A.
THREE	Trace.
FOUR	So.
THREE	As you can imagine.
TWO	Sophie.
THREE	Is having.
FOUR	A.
TWO	Hyper-intellectualised.
THREE	Existential.
FOUR	Crisis.

*

SOPHIE *is with her* GIRLFRIEND.

SOPHIE	I think I'm gonna quit.
GIRLFRIEND	You're not going to quit.
SOPHIE	I'm gonna quit.

GIRLFRIEND	You have, like, three months left, Sophie, that's ridiculous.
SOPHIE	What do they say about toxic relationships? Don't let the sunk time cost keep you in it. Leave.
GIRLFRIEND	Okay?
SOPHIE	My PhD is the toxic relationship.
GIRLFRIEND	I know.
SOPHIE	Not ours.
GIRLFRIEND	I know.
SOPHIE	Maybe I can switch projects, add an extra couple of years. Something with application, in industry, there's always funding for it.
GIRLFRIEND	Do you remember what you told me on our first date?
SOPHIE	That I could see our whole future together already. I stand by that.
GIRLFRIEND	'Application is the lowest aspiration a scientist can have.' You said that.
SOPHIE	Aaaand then you told me you were a doctor.
GIRLFRIEND	Yeah.
SOPHIE	I did pay the bill in apology!

GIRLFRIEND	You did.
SOPHIE	Your point?
GIRLFRIEND	Just that you need to be chasing something new and I need to be holding together what's already there.

*

SOPHIE *meets with her* SUPERVISOR.

SUPERVISOR	Fatigue in the face of an infinite task is very normal, Sophie. You are not the first to feel this way.
SOPHIE	Thank you for understanding.
SUPERVISOR	Oh, I'm not letting you quit, obviously, you have stacks of data sets left. And I won't have you contributing to the leaking pipeline. Women don't leave my teams if I can help it.
SOPHIE	I'm sorry, I think I need to do something else.
SUPERVISOR	When you were only an undergrad you sent me a cold email telling me that in three years you wanted to join this project.
SOPHIE	I know but –
SUPERVISOR	And you came to my office, every fortnight, to try and persuade me to tell you our latest results.
SOPHIE	You never did, though.

SUPERVISOR	Most of the time I didn't have anything to tell. We don't unblind new results every day.
SOPHIE	I know that now.
SUPERVISOR	Sophie, why did you choose physics?
SOPHIE	I was good at maths.
SUPERVISOR	Proper answer please.
SOPHIE	I wanted answers to the questions I thought about most.
SUPERVISOR	And what were those questions?
SOPHIE	Why the stars I'd stay up to watch through the night didn't fall down to Earth.
SUPERVISOR	I didn't know you were a gravity nut.
SOPHIE	I grew out of it once I read Einstein.
SUPERVISOR	At what age?
SOPHIE	Thirteen. When gravity wasn't a mystery anymore I lost interest.
SUPERVISOR	You're working on a mystery now.
SOPHIE	And I'm not sure it has an answer we can find.
SUPERVISOR	I don't need to tell you how coveted this project is. Your position.
SOPHIE	I know.
SUPERVISOR	You weren't the only student

	asking to be considered years before you could apply.
SOPHIE	I know. I'm grateful.
SUPERVISOR	You don't need to be grateful, Sophie. You need to finish your PhD.

*

SOPHIE *with her* GIRLFRIEND.

GIRLFRIEND	Congratulations!
SOPHIE	It's not a congratulations situation.
GIRLFRIEND	Play your cards right and you could win a *Nobel*.
SOPHIE	They don't give Nobel Prizes to PhD students.
GIRLFRIEND	Er. Albert Einstein. Donna Strickland. Frank Wilczek. Didier –
SOPHIE	Um?
GIRLFRIEND	Any fool can digest Wikipedia (!)
SOPHIE	They won it for their *own* work not their supervisor's.
GIRLFRIEND	If your experiment found something, and *you* unblinded the result, you could *very* plausibly lead a new strand of investigation into its properties, and *very* plausibly find something *else*,

	and *very* plausibly write a paper on it that would *very plausibly* get you nominated.
SOPHIE	Right.
GIRLFRIEND	Find a shred of anything about dark matter experimentally and you'll be laughing your way to the podium.
SOPHIE	I think *you* are *very plausibly* full of it.
GIRLFRIEND	Soak it up, Soph. You've got a Schrödinger's cat on your hands here.
SOPHIE	You cannot keep bastardising Schrödinger's cat as *the physics metaphor* for everything.
GIRLFRIEND	Right now, you can live in the dreamy world of possibility where you could be the first person in the world to whom the universe has revealed a new secret.
SOPHIE	I'd prefer to find nothing. At least then the paper will be easier to write.
GIRLFRIEND	Yeah, if writing boring papers is your goal as a scientist.
SOPHIE	What's your 'goal as a scientist', then?
GIRLFRIEND	Firstly, I'm a doctor.

SOPHIE	Still a scientist.
GIRLFRIEND	And secondly, I don't go around with it perfectly phrased in my head all the time, do I?
SOPHIE	Gun to your head.
GIRLFRIEND	To 'dedicate my life to the service of humanity', that's the Declaration of Geneva.
SOPHIE	Lofty.
GIRLFRIEND	You?
SOPHIE	To even get my PhD, the Cambridge Physics Department say I have to make a 'significant contribution to the *creation of new knowledge*'. But it's currently looking like the biggest experiment in human history is going to end with absolutely nothing to show for itself.
GIRLFRIEND	You found the Higgs a decade ago. That was the whole goal.
SOPHIE	It wasn't the *only* goal. There was a goal behind the goal.
GIRLFRIEND	But *you* get to be the person to unblind this last result. Imagine if you get a three sigma.
SOPHIE	It won't be three sigma.

FRIEND	Four sigma would be mind-blowing.
SOPHIE	It's not going to be four sigma.
FRIEND	Five sigma? Front page. Your face. History-making.

*

FOOTNOTE 1. *BREAKING THE MODEL*

All PARTICLES *again.*

A high-hat beat.

This is a vaudeville chant in a four count.

σ

Five sigma, four sigma, three, two, one.

Sigma simply means standard deviation.

Take an average of your data and then you look to see.

How far something is from what you thought it would be.

We test the Standard Model, all the particles we know,

And with each pesky sigma, a tension starts to show.

One tells us nothing, two is no surprise.

But three gets your heart racing, you won't believe your eyes.

The model starts to tremble,

Our knowledge begins to shake

And what we think we know,

    Is bending as to break.

When your data shows five sigma

    It's Nature telling you

    That of all her clueless subjects

    You have found something *new*.

*

We are at CERN, Geneva.

SOPHIE   In Geneva,

    PARTICLES *make snow.*

    deep underground,

    PARTICLES *make darkness.*

    lies the world's largest fridge.
    Otherwise known as
    the cryogenic system of the world's largest
    particle accelerator.

    PARTICLES *make cold.*

    We normally use St Paul's Cathedral
    to explain how deep underground
    our unnatural experiment is.

    It's the height of the cathedral
    plus one more metre.

    A perfect circle so big
    it would take you an hour
    to drive around it in a golf buggy.
    If that was even possible.

    It takes a proton,
    propelled by a loop of
    super-conducting magnets,

just 90 microseconds
to make the same journey.
That's over 11,000 times
a second.

These magnets get so hot
because they are
manipulating the ingredients of nature
in ways that otherwise would
never be seen on Earth.

They bring us as close as we can get
to observing the moments just after
the Big Bang.

When we fire
two beams of protons
directly at one another at this speed,
some 600 million collisions occur
every second.

The average person might have
twelve collisions,
interactions
with other people, a day.
Those might result in the simplest of
outcomes;
a smile in thanks as you board the train
before the kind stranger,
a meeting with a face on a screen,
a bedtime story.

With each collision,
anything can happen,
theoretically.
Your world might fall apart,
you might fall in love.

With 600 million per second,
only one in a million particle interactions
can,
statistically,

be called interesting.

Only those we record.
Only in those,
on a very very rare occasion,
might something
beautiful
happen.

And beauty,
to us physicists,
means something we've never seen before.

We *want* to see this happen.
And so we blind our results.
We shield the region where we expect
to see something beautiful,
in the hope that when we
draw back the veil,
we might find it waiting for us.
We tell ourselves
this makes our results objective.
It tells us we can
trust the beautiful thing is really there
if we see it.

But what if beauty doesn't want to be seen?

If beauty remains a theory,
an illusion we have imagined into
existence,
eluding the limits of our machine.

Then, we need a new machine.

*

SOPHIE *watches a debate between two* PHYSICISTS.

PHYSICIST 1 *is Italian and* PHYSICIST 2 *is German.*

They both speak English.

PHYSICIST 2   You're cutting out.

                PHYSICIST 1 *looks surprised, embarrassed.*

PHYSICIST 1   Sorry.
                I'll start again.
                To answer your question regarding the cost,
                yes,
                thirty billion euro
                is a lot of money.
                But really it isn't.
                It's the cost of a
                cup of coffee
                per year per person
                in every participating nation.
                I'm okay with that as a cost for
                understanding the universe better.
                I can forgo one cappuccino a year.

PHYSICIST 2   And what about
                my question about
                theorised goals?
                The LHC had distinct outcomes
                predicted by the Standard Model.
                The theory of the Higgs' existence
                justified the building of a machine
                to find it
                and we did.
                But all the secondary goals –
                dark matter, supersymmetry –
                that should have *flooded* out behind it,
                never appeared.

                There's no theory this time
                to justify a new machine.
                You can only look for something
                if you have an idea of what it is.

PHYSICIST 1   I'd argue the history of physics is

	full of chance discoveries. The hiss of cosmic background radiation was thought to be the sound of pigeon droppings on a radio telescope, no?
	Nature is right in front of us, we just have to keep looking at it.
PHYSICIST 2	Without theory leading you, you're just fumbling in the dark.
PHYSICIST 1	Sometimes you have to take a leap into the dark to find what you can't yet imagine.
PHYSICIST 2	A thirty billion dollar leap?

*

SOPHIE *and her* GIRLFRIEND.

GIRLFRIEND	I don't mind either way, honestly.
SOPHIE	This decision has mathematical repercussions.
GIRLFRIEND	Not everything is an equation, Sophie.
SOPHIE	Well like, technically, everything can be.
GIRLFRIEND	It's our Deliveroo order.
SOPHIE	They should think about building in the Bellman equation to the app. Give us a value rating based on our ordering history to help us make the optimal mathematical dining decision.

GIRLFRIEND	Some of us don't need to do maths to decide if we want pizza or noodles.
SOPHIE	It's about maximising pay off. It makes sense to order something we *know* we like in the short term. Ramen. How many times have we ordered ramen?
GIRLFRIEND	Maybe every other week since we've been together.
SOPHIE	So, like, fifty-four times. Give or take.
GIRLFRIEND	You don't seriously know how many weeks we've been together off the top of your head.
SOPHIE	Never done us wrong, ramen. But trying something *new* tonight, say –
GIRLFRIEND	Poke bowls?
SOPHIE	Ordering Poke bowls will mostly likely – *and I think this is not just hypothetical in the case of Poke bowls* – end in a less delicious meal.
	In the long run, taking the risk pays off. Our order satisfaction over a number of months or years will go up if we prioritise exploration. In ordering ramen, by exploiting the path of least uncertainty, we are mathematically restricting our ultimate happiness.

GIRLFRIEND	And at what point do we stop exploring? How exactly do you know when you've reached ultimate happiness?
SOPHIE	The thing is I just know I'll hate whatever a Poke bowl is.
GIRLFRIEND	Let's get ramen, then.
SOPHIE	But what if we're missing something better. What's hiding behind the ramen that we can't see? The ramen is the obstacle to greater joy.
GIRLFRIEND	Fine. No ramen.

SOPHIE *abandons the scene.*

*

Back to Geneva.

SOPHIE   The Large Hadron Collider in Geneva
was first proposed in 1984.
Physicists had to wait twenty-six years
to even switch it on.

The *Future* Circular Collider will be
four times as big
and will cost the GDP of a small country
to develop and build.
It is only being proposed
right now.

It will not be ready
to continue the search for new physics
until *2070.*

So after these last results at the LHC,
there will be nothing to do

> but tidy up and listen to
> theorists
> for four
> whole
> decades.
>
> And if we don't end up building the new collider?
> Who knows how long.
>
> Ramen.
> No ramen.
> Either way,
> my career will be
> over before it has even
> begun.

*

The PARTICLES *collapse into* SOPHIE *and another bright collision.*

Energy sparks in all directions, ONE, TWO *and* THREE *rebound and clamber over the bannisters, joining the audience, revealing…*

THE TEACHER
ALEXANDRIA. EGYPT. 415 AD.

...HYPATIA, *a mathematician, philosopher, astronomer, and educator at her lectern.*

TWO	This is Hypatia.
THREE	Hypatia is the most famous polymath in all of Alexandria.
ONE	Hypatia keeps the dying embers of the city's great library alive.
THREE	The library that men built and then subsequently burned by both accident and design.
TWO	Her father is the last director of that great library. After him, it will only exist in memory.
ONE	He is the reason that unlike other girls of her age, she is educated into one of the great minds of her time.
TWO	Her explanatory commentaries

	are the reason you can look at the skies and predict what you will see.
ONE	The reason you can draw the path of a planet with minute accuracy.
THREE	The reason you can simplify the universe into an equation of symbols.
ONE	Hypatia is a genius.
TWO	Hypatia is worshipped.
THREE	Hypatia is a *woman*.
TWO	So, as you can imagine.
THREE	For the powerful *men* of her city.
TWO	Hypatia.
ONE	Is provoking.
TWO	An.
ONE	Existential.
THREE	Crisis.

*

A lecture hall full of eager STUDENTS.

| HYPATIA | You'll find a piece of papyrus and a stylus
on your desks
would you be so kind as to
Pick.
Those. |

THE TEACHER 33

Up.
You can share if you've managed
to drop yours under your feet already.

*A small whiteboard and a blue dry-wipe
marker have been on every desk/seat since
the beginning.*

STUDENT 1   I haven't got any!

STUDENT 2   I have spare.

HYPATIA   Of course you do, Flavius.

Help him and anyone else, please.

STUDENT 2 *gives a whiteboard and pen
to* STUDENT 1 *and anyone else who is
struggling to find theirs.*

Once you have your instruments in hand,
I would like you all to draw
a small circle,
the size of your thumbnail,
in the middle of your canvas.

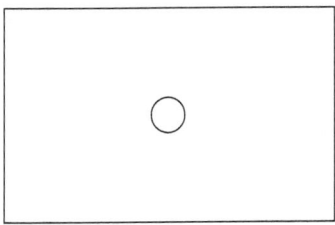

If I told you that circle was
the centre of the universe,
what would it be?

STUDENT 3   What's her name, Atilius?

STUDENT 2   *Lucia*, isn't it?

STUDENT 3   The centre of Atilius' universe
               is called Lucia.

HYPATIA	Perhaps the centre of *your* universe is *your current girlfriend*, Atilius –
STUDENT 3	He wishes! She doesn't even know he exists.
HYPATIA	– but for the rest of us, it's the Earth. It's all of us, including your Lucia.

Now, surrounding your Earth,
please draw another eight circles,
encompassing those drawn before it,
each slightly larger than the last.
It should look like the cross section of a tree.

Concentric rings
around your central circle,
growing to fill the page.

When you have nine circles in total,
including the one at the centre,
you have finished.

Show me.

HYPATIA *responds to the drawings in the room.*

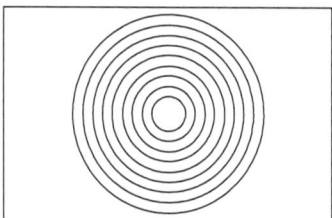

Then:

Congratulations, class.
You have just drawn

	the entire universe as we know it.
	A distant and threatening sound outside begins.
STUDENT 3	Flavius, you've drawn yours upside down.
HYPATIA	You can't draw a circle upside down, Maximus.
STUDENT 2	Is this incorrect?
	STUDENT 2 *shows their drawing.*
HYPATIA	How many times have you attended this lecture, Flavius?
STUDENT 2	Seven.
HYPATIA	So you can tell us what the rings represent on your immaculate diagram.
STUDENT 3	Get it wrong and you're committing blasphemy.
HYPATIA	In this school, I'm the authority, Maximus. Not your father's church.
STUDENT 3	Oh yeah?
HYPATIA	Yes. And your own circles are a bit wonky from what I can see. Flavius?
	The danger outside grows more menacing.
STUDENT 2	The first ring is the orbit of the moon. The ring around that the path of Mercury. Then Venus. Then the Sun.
STUDENT 3	I have a question about the Sun.

HYPATIA	It can wait.
STUDENT 3	I've been reading Aristarchus' theory of Heliocentrism.
HYPATIA	You and every other twenty-one-year-old who wants a political career.
STUDENT 3	Why don't you teach it?
HYPATIA	Because it's been a hundred years since he dreamed it up and we still cannot detect a sign of the stellar parallax it would imply. The stars aren't moving, which means the Earth isn't either.
STUDENT 3	That we can see.
HYPATIA	And until we invent better eyes than those in our heads, Maximus, I'm afraid this is the best model we have and it is the model I will teach. Flavius?
STUDENT 2	The last four rings are the orbits of Mars, Jupiter, and Saturn. Then last of all, the ninth circle, the firmament of stars.
HYPATIA	Very good.
	Earth. Moon. Mercury. Venus. Sun. Mars. Jupiter. Saturn. Stars.
	This is the model Ptolemy gave us two hundred and fifty years ago. And it has accurately predicted

	the motion of celestial bodies ever since.
STUDENT 1	How?
	HYPATIA *asks someone on the front row:*
HYPATIA	Throw me your pen.
	We hope they throw it.
	We hope HYPATIA *catches it.*
	With an arc like *that*. If this pen is a planet, you threw it at its earliest observation, it moved through an orbit, and I caught it at –
STUDENT 3	What good is a teacher if her philosophy is to stick to the past instead of embracing the future?
	The danger outside is overwhelming.
HYPATIA	There is no future without the past, Maximus.
STUDENT 3	I can hear your future at the door.
HYPATIA	And you can see me after class.

*

Suddenly, silence.

HYPATIA *and* STUDENT 3 *alone.*

| HYPATIA | Was that a threat?
You're going to have to forget you're the son of a bishop.
Who you are does not matter here. |
| STUDENT 3 | Sorry. I'm having trouble
with my algebra. |

HYPATIA	So you provoked me into calling you behind (?)
STUDENT 3	I can't have the others know. Who'll vote for a man who can't master basic calculus.
HYPATIA	Tell me what age the great Diophantus died.
STUDENT 3	I don't know. He was old, though.
HYPATIA	You can work it out.

An equation appears above STUDENT 3*'s head as* HYPATIA *speaks:*

$$\frac{x}{6} + \frac{x}{12} + \frac{x}{7} + 5 + \frac{x}{2} + 4 = x$$

His boyhood lasted a sixth of his life;
his beard grew after a twelfth more;
after a seventh more he married,
and his son was born five years later;
the son lived to half his father's age,
and the father died four years after his son.

Tomorrow,
bring me the answer.
The age he died.

STUDENT 3	I can give it to you now, just give me a minute.
HYPATIA	No, I have more work at home. In fact, I think your father has requested a meeting about the bridge he wants to build.
STUDENT 3	Don't leave, Hypatia.
HYPATIA	Why?
STUDENT 3	Don't walk out those doors. Don't get into your carriage. They're –

HYPATIA	Goodnight, Maximus.

*

*We are momentarily back in **2026**.*

SOPHIE *is at the university library consulting a* LIBRARIAN *with her glasses on a chain.*

LIBRARIAN *is preferably Scottish.*

SOPHIE	H. Y. P.
LIBRARIAN	I know how to spell it.
SOPHIE	There's no N on the end. Hypati<u>a</u>. *a.*
	Death stare from LIBRARIAN.
LIBRARIAN	Thank you.
SOPHIE	Is there anything I can see today?
LIBRARIAN	There's not much left of her, that I can see. But you're best off starting with the letters, there's fourteen fragments in all –
SOPHIE	I'd like to read them all please.
LIBRARIAN	Okay. They'll be ready for you tomorrow.
SOPHIE	I can't read them now?
LIBRARIAN	Libraries don't run on magic. Someone has to travel to the belly of the earth and back to fetch them from the storeroom.
SOPHIE	Sorry.

LIBRARIAN	If you're in a hurry, there will be inferior translations you can consult online. Just don't come crying to me when your supervisor sneers at your bibliography.

*

A computer screen glares light onto SOPHIE*'s face.*

HYPATIA *reappears behind her.*

They speak through millennia.

SOPHIE	God, is this really all there is left of you?
HYPATIA	A philosopher is only as good as her questions. You'll need to be more specific.
SOPHIE	Why aren't you writing your own stuff? Why are you just teaching?
HYPATIA	Because it is necessary.
SOPHIE	To sacrifice your own work for a duty to preserving others'?
HYPATIA	Not duty, *beauty*.
	If we want to live in a beautiful world, full of beautiful ideas, beautiful structures, *someone must do the work.*
SOPHIE	Would you still give the lecture if you knew what it would cost you?

The PARTICLES *bind* SOPHIE*'s hands behind her back.*

*

FOOTNOTE 2. *THE COST*

TWO	You're giving a lecture. It's popular, like all your lectures.
THREE	It's late, and even as you finish more men are arriving, having heard you were speaking somewhere in the city.
TWO	A crowd gathers outside and as you approach the doors to leave, they hush in the hope of a few words.
THREE	The night air is fresh and cold against your cheeks, flushed from the excitement of a room full of intelligent questions.
TWO	Your students cling to your robes, requesting clarifications on the ideas you presented tonight. Their hands support you into your carriage and deposit letters full of admiration, ardour, and inquiry on the seat beside you.
THREE	The carriage starts to move and you open the first. It is from him, again, a student you taught a decade ago, now running a province abroad. He asks why you have not replied in weeks, months.

	Sickness has taken his children and he longs to hear from you.
TWO	The next is from the newly elected archon, requesting an audience to consult your assessment of the city's political tensions.
THREE	The next contains only a torn piece of fabric, stained with what looks like blood.
TWO	The carriage stops. It is quiet on the road. Your students are far behind and their questions faded into the night.
THREE	The door opens. Hands reaching, and you feel the cold air once more. Bodies everywhere and a weight pushing on your shoulders. Colder still as fabric is torn and the letters in your hands fall like heavy snow to the ground.
TWO	The pain begins. Sharp and solid slices to the skin. Projectiles from all sides. Bruising, breaking, bombing until your knees give and your cheek stings as dust dirties a fresh wound.
THREE	The light of the moon fades as bodies block your view to the sky.

| | You train your eyes through the
gap between their heads to
find one flickering light.
One star on which to
fix your gaze. |
|-------|---|
| TWO | When it is over,
in pieces,
they take you to a temple
on the waterfront,
looking out from the city. |
| THREE | And as the sun rises,
and the stars recede,
they celebrate your demise
with your own
ritual. |
| TWO | They light a fire and
turn you to
ash.
Laughing
as the smoke turns
white. |
| THREE | You can't know
that a man
passed the crowded street outside your
lecture
an hour before.
That he had asked
who these hundreds of men were
so desperate to hear speak.
That he had received
your name in answer. |
| TWO | You can't know
that he was so struck with jealousy,
he turned to his followers and
ordered this. |

THREE	That *he* will be made a Saint once centuries are passed and the bloodstains long faded.
TWO	You can't know that when men write about *you,* they will spend *one sentence* describing your mind, and *paragraphs* describing your murder.
THREE	The sordid details of a violent death and the machinations of the feuding men who caused it.
TWO	You can't know that your murder will become the singular marker of your life.
THREE	The smudge.
TWO	The hint of your work.
THREE	You can't know this is the cost.
TWO	The cost of a woman pulling a thread in the fabric of the universe.

*

HYPATIA *and* SOPHIE *again.*

HYPATIA	I would still give the lecture. Knowing the cost.

SOPHIE	Were you not afraid to die?
HYPATIA	I believe death is twofold. First: the body liberated from the soul. Second: the soul from the body. One does not necessarily follow the other. I find that a very interesting idea. Not a frightening one.
	And I died doing what I love. Looking at the stars.
	HYPATIA *falls into the darkness of history.*

*

*Back in **2026**.*

GIRLFRIEND *is home after a night shift, and finds* SOPHIE *glued to her computer.*

SOPHIE	But you have to read this stuff for yourself. It's online. Bad translations though.
GIRLFRIEND	How would you know? You don't read Greek.
SOPHIE	I can tell now. From all the ones I've read. What's a good translation.
GIRLFRIEND	Do you know it's 6am?
SOPHIE	Yeah.
GIRLFRIEND	Have you slept, Sophie?
SOPHIE	My supervisor told me to seek inspiration.
GIRLFRIEND	I thought letting you unblind the results was meant to do that.

SOPHIE	That just made me feel worse. She told me to research women in maths. Women in physics.
GIRLFRIEND	Why?
SOPHIE	To feel… akin. Part of something.
GIRLFRIEND	So do you?
SOPHIE	The thing is, if people have written articles about you, you must have discovered something huge, *created new knowledge,* reformed our understanding of the universe. Whereas I have ramen encrusted into my hair.
GIRLFRIEND	Maybe get some sleep.
SOPHIE	How was your shift?
GIRLFRIEND	Awful. Had a death this morning.
SOPHIE	God, I'm sorry. Why didn't you say?
GIRLFRIEND	Maybe because the second I got in, you sat me down and started telling me about a brutal murder of some poor woman in Egypt.
SOPHIE	It's what the story *means,* though.
GIRLFRIEND	That you're lucky you won't be stoned to death for getting a PhD? That you won't burst into flames when you unblind the result? That seems like a lowest-common-denominator consolation to me.

SOPHIE	It's a *symbol*, her murder.
It tells us so little about her
but it's all we have to go on.
And that's exactly how we use the collider.
We look for a signature of something
far more complex and interesting than we
could ever predict, known only by
the mark it leaves
behind.
GIRLFRIEND	Fascinating.
I'm going to bed.
SOPHIE	Doesn't it
bother you?
GIRLFRIEND	That a woman was murdered
sixteen hundred years ago?
Yes that bothers me.
SOPHIE	That you go to work,
come home,
eat a bowl of pasta,
sleep, maybe go for a run,
watch four episodes of *Real Housewives*,
over and over,
when all the while you have
no idea how you're able to do all that.
No idea what's even holding you and I in
the same room.
Why we aren't hurtling away from one
another
at the speed of light.
GIRLFRIEND	I've been on call for twelve hours,
Soph, can we not do the
physics –
SOPHIE	Well it's not *love,* is it?
GIRLFRIEND	What?

SOPHIE	It's way more important than that. It's gravity. Specifically gravity caused by the thing *I'm trying to find.*
GIRLFRIEND	And what exactly is the difference between love and gravity, Sophie?
SOPHIE	Gravity is nature and love is something we've invented to give nature meaning.
GIRLFRIEND	I don't think you believe that.
SOPHIE	It doesn't matter what I *believe.* Nature is nature.
GIRLFRIEND	Are you coming to bed?
SOPHIE	I'm not finished.

GIRLFRIEND and SOPHIE *turn away from each other but the* PARTICLES *catch them and swing the two of them into a collision of darkness.*

A small light illuminates what is left behind...

THE MEDIUM
HACKNEY. LONDON. 1874 AD.

...FLORENCE, *fifteen, a notorious medium.*

The PARTICLES whisper over a hymn playing on a piano:

ONE	This is Florence.
THREE	Ever since Florence was a little girl, she has heard the voices of angels speaking to her.
FOUR	At fifteen, Florence conducts a séance with her friends and a table lifts high into the air.
ONE	So Florence is under scientific investigation.
THREE	Because Florence has developed a peculiar capacity to conjure the dead.
TWO	She is the conductive material

	and the spirits are the current flowing through her.
THREE	All around her, humanity witnesses the invisible becoming visible.
ONE	Electricity is animating the world anew.
FOUR	Messages pass through the air.
ONE	Sparks flare from nothingness.
FOUR	It is a strange time to be alive.
ONE	And men of science.
FOUR	Are straining to decide.
ONE	If the dead are really talking to the living.
THREE	Or if this girl is just having.
FOUR	A.
ONE	Particularly *eccentric*.
THREE	Existential.
FOUR	Crisis.

*

FOOTNOTE 3. *THE LAWS OF A SÉANCE*

Three Victorian gentlemen puffing their pipes under a streetlamp.

Exaggerated RP accents.

GENTLEMAN 1	Before we go in, are we all crystal clear?
GENTLEMAN 3	As a microscope, Sir.
GENTLEMAN 1	Repeat it back to me. I want zero interference with my observations.
GENTLEMAN 3	Rule Number One: No skeptics.
GENTLEMAN 2	'*Why would a spirit waste their time with the unbelieving?*' It's a convenient argument for skeptic and sympathetic alike.
GENTLEMAN 1	*Watch it.* Rule Number Two?
GENTLEMAN 3	No turning the lights on.
GENTLEMAN 1	At risk of?
GENTLEMAN 3	Damaging the medium.
GENTLEMAN 1	Why?
GENTLEMAN 3	The ectoplasmic material of the manifestation will rush back to her own body, unconscious behind the curtain, with such force as to kill her.
GENTLEMAN 2	Only in the dark is she kept safe from harm *(or real scrutiny).*
GENTLEMAN 1	And most importantly?
GENTLEMAN 3	Rule Number Three: No touching.

GENTLEMAN 2	I'm sure we don't need to explain that one.
GENTLEMAN 1	The three Nos. No. No. No. Just sit there and take it in like a good scientist.
GENTLEMAN 3	What do I do if *she* touches *me??*
GENTLEMAN 1	Steady on, boy.
GENTLEMAN 2	I remember my first séance.
GENTLEMAN 1	You *let* her. Just keep your hands on the table where we can see them.

*

GENTLEMAN 1 *catches a top hat and becomes* WILLIAM CROOKES.

He draws a curled moustache on his face.

CROOKES	William Crookes. Inventor of an instrument that will enable the discovery of the electron. Certified genius. GENTLEMAN 3 *becomes* ARTHUR CONAN DOYLE. *He draws himself a zig-zag moustache.*
DOYLE	On his left, Arthur Conan Doyle, creator of the most famous fictional detective of all time. Certified genius.

	GENTLEMAN 2 *becomes* HARRY HOUDINI.
	DOYLE *draws him a super spiral moustache.*
HOUDINI	On *his* left, Harry Houdini. The most famous illusionist of all time.
	Certified genius.
DOYLE	A chemist, an author, and a magician walk into a *bar*.
HOUDINI	A *drawing room*.
CROOKES	A *séance*.
HOUDINI	To marvel at a fifteen-year-old girl.
CROOKES	Certification pending.

*

The dark drawing room of a small house in Hackney.

We are inside FLORENCE*'s head.*

FLORENCE	I can feel his pulse as he takes mine. The steady rhythm of a scientific mind at work.
	He kisses my hand and bows his head. I wait for him to lift his eyes back to mine. I never know what to say in these moments before.

The lights are dimmed,
the chairs are arranged,
the circle forms.
My sister plays the piano in
a dark corner.

They are ready.
He is ready.
And so am I.

Inside a spirit cabinet.

Inside, he ties me to the chair
himself. The knots are tight but
his placement is kind.
He doesn't want me to be
uncomfortable, he says,
but I tell him to bind it
tighter.

I'm not afraid to be tested.

A longing look as
he disappears through the door
and shuts it behind him,
leaving me and taking with him
all the light in the world.

I close my eyes and
give myself to
her.

FLORENCE *experiences a violent change.*

It starts in my toes.
A burning.
No pain but the
lick of flames
coaxing the matter of my body
to melting.

The heat travels up the
back of my legs and seizes

my lower back.
I arch, and the chair
digs into my shoulder blades.

It's everywhere.
My neck is ablaze and
my face burns, the blood
drawn to the surface by the
magnetism of her
presence.

FLORENCE*'s body pours ectoplasm.*

The very fibres of my body
begin to change.
To liquify.
To pour from every orifice.

A sound I do not recognise
tries to escape my lips, but
there is no breath to carry it.
I am not breathing any more.

She is.

FLORENCE *becomes* KATIE, *twenty-four, the notorious daughter of an even more notorious pirate. She is now dressed in white, is paler, and her hair has changed colour.*

She speaks differently.

Her black dress lies on the floor next to her, like a lifeless body.

KATIE I look down on
poor Florence,
unconscious and
slumped, held up by
the ropes that bind her.
Such a young girl to carry so
heavy a burden as this gift.

	So young, and so mutable.
	I turn the handle of the cabinet door. Pull back the curtain. I hear an intake of breath.
	I step into the flicker of the lamp's flame to see the face of a man who can't believe his eyes.
HOUDINI	I can't believe my eyes (!)
KATIE	And yet he does.

*

We are inside CROOKES*'s head.*

KATIE *gives silent messages to members of the audience, flirts with them, frightens them.*

CROOKES	As the spirit moves closer to our electric light, I notice the marks I saw moments ago on Florence's face are nowhere on this Katie's.
	She takes my hand and holds it to her neck, where an impossible warmth radiates.
	I cut a lock from her auburn tresses; a soft proof of her.
	We are inside DOYLE*'s head.*
DOYLE	I thought the medium's hair had been so dark brown as to appear *black*

when she entered the cabinet.
Such a change has occurred as to
strike me
dumb.

The spirit may have been with us
for a few minutes or an hour.
I cannot tell.
She holds us transfixed
with her darting gaze,
her piercing laugh,

KATIE *laughs, piercingly.*

her deep voice telling stories
of the high seas.

When at last she turns back
towards the cabinet,
she clears her throat.

KATIE *coughs gently and shakes her mane of hair.*

KATIE

Tonight will be my last visit on this earth.
Our work is over.
We have provided
evidence enough.

DOYLE

A sound like
a gull passing over shore
leaves William's throat.

All eyes follow this gull above.

Poor fellow is in love.

HOUDINI

Behind his back,
his colleagues raise their eyebrows.
'William's girl', they call her.

But this is indeed a sort of love story
I have witnessed tonight.

>   Between a girl and
>   the power she wields over
>   this man of
>   science.

*

2026.

SOPHIE *is with the* LIBRARIAN *again.*

LIBRARIAN	Back so soon?
SOPHIE	There was only a few short accounts. Mostly about her death.
LIBRARIAN	Don't shoot the messenger. Blame the sands of time.
SOPHIE	I'd like to read her commentaries. I'd like to read anything she would have read and anything she might have written about.
LIBRARIAN	What was her name again?
SOPHIE	How many times? Hypatia.

*

CROOKES *presents his report.*

CROOKES	I wish to make the most public acknowledgment of the obligations I am under to Miss Florence, for every test I have proposed she has at once agreed to submit.

*

In a different realm, SOPHIE *tells a story.*

THE MEDIUM 59

SOPHIE
So there's this cave
and deep inside are a group of men,
so deep that they are in total darkness
and they've been there since birth.
Oh, and they're chained up
so they can't leave.

*

CROOKES
To imagine
that an innocent schoolgirl of fifteen
should be able to conceive and then
successfully carry out for three years
so gigantic an imposture as this
does more violence to one's common sense
than to believe her to be what the
evidence affirms.

*

SOPHIE
And behind these men in the cave is a fire,
throwing their shadows on the wall of rock,
so that all they know of the world are those
dark shapes dancing in front of them.

And the thought experiment is to say that
one day, one of those men
finds his chains loose and is able to
turn around. What if he escapes
and climbs to the cave's mouth to
stand in the light of the sun?
He is blinded by it.

*

CROOKES
The spirit, Katie, even consented to
testing a full light upon her image.
She stood arms extended as if
crucified.

	KATIE *begins to disintegrate.*
	She looked like herself for the space of a second only, then she began to melt, dematerialising like a wax doll melting before a hot fire.
HOUDINI	First, her features became blurred and indistinct; they seemed to run into each other.
CROOKES	The eyes sunk in their sockets, the nose disappeared, the frontal bone fell in.
HOUDINI	Next, the limbs appeared to give way under her, and she sank lower and lower on the carpet, like a crumbling edifice.
CROOKES	At last there was nothing but her head. Then a heap of white drapery only, which disappeared with a whisk, as if a hand had pulled it after her.
	We were left staring at the spot on which the spirit Katie King had stood.
	A whip of white and KATIE *disappears entirely.*

*

SOPHIE	And when the man finally becomes accustomed to the light, he beholds the world; mountains, rivers, animals, celestial bodies

>   that his mind could never have imagined
>   chained up in the dark.
>   He has been shown the true reality of the
>   world.
>   So he runs back down the passage of the
>   cave
>   to describe to his friends everything he has
>   seen,
>   painting as vivid a picture as he can.

*

FLORENCE *and* CROOKES *face one another, one last time:*

FLORENCE   Was it enough?

CROOKES   You know, I think it was.
           It will have convinced
           the great majority of people,
           who know anything about the subject,
           of the existence of the
           next world.

*

The GENTLEMEN *again for a moment.*

GENTLEMAN 2   Have you read this?

GENTLEMAN 3   Twice.
              To make sure my eyes weren't failing me.

GENTLEMAN 2   Bonkers.

GENTLEMAN 3   Right.
              Pull the other one, Crookes.

*

2026.

SOPHIE *has been telling her* GIRLFRIEND *a story as they brush their teeth.*

SOPHIE   And they don't believe a word he says.
           They refuse his offer to break their chains
           and,

> not wanting to leave their company,
> the enlightened man sits back down and
> keeps what he knows to himself.
>
> And before long, the picture fades
> from his own mind. The
> illusion of shadows
> becomes his whole world again.
> Humanity remains
> in the darkness.

.

GIRLFRIEND: That's depressing.

SOPHIE: Yeah,
it's Plato.

GIRLFRIEND: And I suppose
you're the enlightened man?

SOPHIE: No, I'm one of the men
in the cave.

GIRLFRIEND: You can hardly call
your fully funded PhD
a *chain around your neck,* Sophie.

SOPHIE: My first year
I spent 80% of my time
underground at the collider.
Didn't see daylight for
months.

GIRLFRIEND: You loved being at CERN.

SOPHIE: But if I *was* the enlightened man,
if I discovered the true reality of things,
you sure wouldn't catch me
running back into the cave.

GIRLFRIEND: You'd keep all the knowledge
to yourself?

SOPHIE: Versus losing it entirely? Sure.

	I'd rather know something no-one else does,
	than not know it just because they don't.
GIRLFRIEND	I don't think that's what Plato is getting at.
SOPHIE	No, he's saying we're all
	victims of our perceptions.
	We take only what's
	right in front of our noses
	to be the entirety of reality.
GIRLFRIEND	But also –
SOPHIE	And of course,
	in response,
	he's proselytising that the search for
	true knowledge is –
GIRLFRIEND	Isn't he suggesting that
	being in the dark and
	not knowing the full extent of things is
	our natural place in the universe?
	That the evolution of human knowledge
	is a
	journey through a *sequence* of caves,
	each a little bit bigger,
	revealing a little bit more,
	but never the
	full picture?
SOPHIE	Perpetual darkness?
GIRLFRIEND	The enlightened man isn't satisfied,
	even when he's seen the light.
	That's what Plato means.
	No matter what shiny new things
	you get to discover,
	it'll never be enough for you.
SOPHIE	When did this become about
	me?

GIRLFRIEND Which am I, then?
A chain around your neck or
the light at the top of the tunnel that
you leave behind.

>GIRLFRIEND *attempts to leave the scene, but a collision pulls her to the centre as an orchestra starts to tune. The* PARTICLES *wake up backstage of a theatre; they rebound in a flurry...*

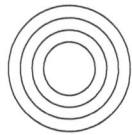

THE MAGICIAN
NEW YORK CITY. 1897 AD.

...and a begrudging THREE *is pushed onto the podium, she is still* GIRLFRIEND.

ONE	This is Adelaide.
GIRLFRIEND	What?
TWO	At eighteen, a magician makes Adelaide's engagement ring disappear and reappear before her eyes.
FOUR	When Adelaide boards a ship bound for America she finds that same magician smoking on the deck, smiling at her.
ONE	By the time they reach land, she decides to marry him instead. Partners in life and in magic.
	ONE *whisks* GIRLFRIEND *off the platform and replaces her.*
GIRLFRIEND	Sophie??
FOUR	He teaches her all his secrets and she teaches him all her charm.

ONE	From Rio de Janeiro to St Petersburg they perform the impossible.
TWO	For Czars and Queens, she is shot from a cannon, levitated, and burned in a pillar of fire. Always emerging safe, smiling, and sensationally attired.
FOUR	The world simply cannot get enough.
TWO	Until her husband dies on a train, cigarette in hand, leaving a fortune of debt and a legacy to uphold.
ONE	Leaving Adelaide to hold the stage alone.

The PARTICLES *push* THREE *back onto the podium.*

THREE *slowly becomes* ADELAIDE.

ADELAIDE	A one-woman show.
TWO	In an age when one-woman shows aren't really a thing.
FOUR	She decides to perform the very trick she forbade of her husband.
ONE	A trick that kills magicians by the dozen.
TWO	So that after tonight, she will be called the 'Queen of Magic'.
ADELAIDE	Really?

FOUR	But first.
	Showtime positions.
TWO	In front of a thousand people.
ONE	She must survive.
TWO	A.
ONE	Very Literal.
FOUR	Existential.
ONE	Crisis.
FOUR	At gunpoint.
	ADELAIDE *gulps.*

*

Two bros of the FIRING SQUAD *in a spotlight.*

Thick New York accents.

A drumroll.

FIRING SQ. 1	I'm nervous.
FIRING SQ. 2	What do you have to be nervous about? It's a trick.
FIRING SQ. 1	Do you know how she does it?
FIRING SQ. 2	Er, yeah, I have an idea.
FIRING SQ. 1	Go on.
FIRING SQ. 2	Sleight of hand, isn't it.
FIRING SQ. 1	But how exactly is it sleight of hand? Go on.

FIRING SQ. 2	Alright fine, I don't know. But it's not our job to.
FIRING SQ. 1	I'd feel a lot better if I understood it.
FIRING SQ. 2	It makes it more real. Your being nervous adds to the spectacle. The risk. Even the firing squad don't know what might happen. The audience can feel that tension.
FIRING SQ. 1	If something *did* happen? If the bullet I fired – ?
FIRING SQ. 2	Then it'd be the best show they ever seen. And we wouldn't have to clean up the mess. It's says so in our contracts.

*

FOOTNOTE 4. *SCHRÖDINGER'S BULLET*

The PARTICLES *become bullets in their guns.*

TWO	It all rests on a single moment. The entire trick.
THREE	And it's all in the bullets themselves.
FOUR	That's us. The bullets. Loaded in a rifle.
ONE	One in each gun.

THREE	Four guns in a line.
TWO	Pointing at Adelaide's head.
ONE	Fingers on triggers.
FOUR	A wink.
TWO	And they fire.
THREE	Trusting that at some point.
ONE	The live bullets marked with initials.
TWO	Have been swapped.
FOUR	For blanks.
THREE	But how, you ask?
ONE	Adelaide is metres away!
TWO	We'll tell you how…
FOUR	The key is in the distraction –

*

The gunfire cuts them off.

The sound of four bullets hitting a china plate. Ting. Ting. Ting. Ting.

The flash of a shutter camera.

The flurry of success.

JOURNALIST 1	'Although there are a great many exponents of the art of sleight-of-hand of the masculine gender,

> there are not over many
> *female* mystifiers.
> One of the latest to arrive in London is
> Madame Herrmann,
> widow of the late great magician.'

JOURNALIST 2 'Adelaide Herrmann,
widow of Herrmann the Great,
is keeping his fame alive.
She mystifies and astonishes
as did her husband,
the greatest magician
of modern times.'

*

ADELAIDE *is taking her tea, reading the papers over breakfast.*

So is her useless nephew, LEO HERRMANN.

ADELAIDE Yes, the seventeen minute
standing ovation
would say as much.

LEO HERRMANN Yes, Aunt.

ADELAIDE How many times did
my dearest Alexander
ever perform
the Bullet Catch in
one show?

LEO HERRMANN Once, Aunt.

ADELAIDE Once.
Like everyone else.
Even doing it once
is extraordinary.
And I did it?

LEO HERRMANN Six times, Aunt.

ADELAIDE Six times.
Six!
On the trot.

	And all I get are comparisons.
LEO HERRMANN	This one's better:

*

JOURNALIST 3	'While a new *'Queen of Magic'* has asserted herself in the form of Adelaide Herrmann, a different kind of manifestation – just as unbelievable and mysterious – is taking place in the séances occurring in modest drawing rooms across the world, tested rigorously by our best scientific minds.'

*

ADELAIDE *snatches the paper.*

ADELAIDE	'Woman Astounds Psychic Experts.' What a load of *nonsense*.
LEO HERRMANN	I've been to one. Looked pretty real to me.
ADELAIDE	Leo. Do my shows look real to you?
LEO HERRMANN	Of course, Aunt. You're a master of illusion.
ADELAIDE	Exactly. These young *mediums* are nothing different. Masters of those same illusions, but for illicit ends.
LEO HERRMANN	Yes, Aunt.

ADELAIDE   I'd like to meet one of these charlatans.

*

2026.

SOPHIE *and her* GIRLFRIEND

SOPHIE   I have to go I'm meeting my supervisor.

GIRLFRIEND   You can't say you have a meeting every time I start a conversation you don't like.

SOPHIE   I've literally had this meeting every week for the past –

*

Simultaneously, SOPHIE *and her* SUPERVISOR

SUPERVISOR   I don't buy it, Sophie.
This tortured physicist
act.

SOPHIE   It's not an act,
I'm having a really
hard time.

*

GIRLFRIEND   Am I living up to it?

SOPHIE   What?

GIRLFRIEND   The future of ours you conjured up on our first date.

SOPHIE   We're in it. This is that future.

*

SUPERVISOR   A breakup is
no reason to pass over an
opportunity like this.

SOPHIE	It's actually not a break*up* it's more of an indefinite –

*

GIRLFRIEND	I don't want to have my whole life mapped out for me by someone else.
SOPHIE	It's a *nice* thing to say to someone. That you could imagine being with them forever.
GIRLFRIEND	Not if it becomes the only sure thing they cling to. That they hold you to.
SOPHIE	I'm not holding you to anything!

*

SUPERVISOR	Sophie, did you do as I suggested?
SOPHIE	Yes.
SUPERVISOR	And do you feel better about the unblinding?
SOPHIE	I do.
SUPERVISOR	Fantastic!
SOPHIE	Because I've realised nothing matters and nothing we can do can make a difference to that.
SUPERVISOR	Okay, that's not exactly what I –

*

GIRLFRIEND	You're holding me to an idea of a future that I don't have any say in.
SOPHIE	That's ridiculous.

*

SUPERVISOR	*Sophie.*

*

GIRLFRIEND	*My* future. Built on *my* present, which is just as important as yours.
SOPHIE	I know that.
GIRLFRIEND	Do you?
SOPHIE	Yes. Obviously your present is important to you.
GIRLFRIEND	But yours is important to, what, the whole universe?
SOPHIE	Well, actually, yeah, kind of.
GIRLFRIEND	Can you hear yourself? What do you think happens when you stake this much of yourself on the worst bet in human history.

*

SOPHIE	Tomorrow, when I press the key on our computer, there will be no possibility left.
SUPERVISOR	All realities collapse into one.
SOPHIE	I like the certainty of that. An end.
SUPERVISOR	You said you were quitting three months ago and you're still here. I don't think you're looking for an ending, Sophie.

*

SOPHIE   For the last four years,
                      this experiment has been the
                      only thing I talk about.
                      The way I filter meaning
                      from every interaction I have.
                      The flimsy sense of purpose
                      I cling to just because I can say
                      we are on the cusp of something.

                      But being on the cusp
                      continually is actually just
                      completely exhausting and
                      by definition is not ever the
                      discovery of the thing itself.

                      A never-ending fumble in the dark,
                      hopelessly failing to find the answer
                      that is right in front of us,
                      but always out of reach.

                      We might as well be at the
                      very beginning.

*

ADELAIDE *takes the mic.*

She throws FLORENCE *onto the podium.*

ADELAIDE   Ladies and Gentleman,
                      what has been observed
                      in these séances is no miracle.
                      There is no ectoplasm.
                      There is no spirit.

                      This is just a little girl
                      putting on a strange little show
                      in her drawing rooms,
                      exploiting the anxieties of
                      her dutifully paying audience.

                      SOPHIE *unplugs the mic.*

*

SOPHIE	And you don't exploit yours?
ADELAIDE	My audiences agree to a deception.
FLORENCE	And mine are open to what is beyond their understanding.
ADELAIDE	It's fraud.
FLORENCE	It's real to the people in the room.
ADELAIDE	Who wouldn't want it to be real? To talk to a loved one they had lost.
FLORENCE	Would you like to speak to yours?
ADELAIDE	I don't need an experiment to know you've built your reputation on nothing more than profound gullibility. So-called 'proof' burns bright and fast back into nothingness.
SOPHIE	Just like you. Your shows turned out to be as flammable as your act pretended they were. It all literally turns to ash.
ADELAIDE	You can't burn away seventy years.
SOPHIE	What use is a 'Queen of Magic' when no-one can make a fortune from her stuff? I've never even heard of you.
FLORENCE	You could say, Adelaide, that the greatest trick you ever pulled off was your disappearing act from the pages of history.

ADELAIDE *disappears.*

FLORENCE *and* SOPHIE *remain.*

So you believe me?

SOPHIE	I only believe in what I can observe.
FLORENCE	And how about what you can *feel*?
	FLORENCE *disappears.*

*

GIRLFRIEND	I'm unhappy, Sophie. I'm trying to tell you I'm not happy. And that has nothing to do with the outcome of your experiment but everything to do with how you make me feel like it does.
SOPHIE	Is it dead or alive, then?
GIRLFRIEND	What?
SOPHIE	The cat.
GIRLFRIEND	*Sophie.*
SOPHIE	The cat is us.
	GIRLFRIEND *leaves.*

*

SUPERVISOR	Why do you think I accepted you onto this team, Sophie?
SOPHIE	I don't know, because I hounded you for three years?
SUPERVISOR	Nope.
SOPHIE	Because I came first in my year and had a reference from the head of department?
SUPERVISOR	Irrelevant.
SOPHIE	Because I was the only woman who applied?

SUPERVISOR I hired you because of
one line you wrote in your application.
The very same line you wrote in your first
email to me.

Do you remember what it was?

*A super collision. We are transported to
the dark side of the universe...*

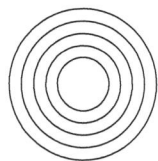

THE ASTRONOMER

...something about the world should be revealed as fundamentally different to what we have assumed so far, something that can't be unseen once it has been revealed.

The PARTICLES *tell us a story.*

They describe an invisible woman.

ONE	This is Vera.
	Maybe they conjure her from nothing.
THREE	As a little girl, she climbs over her snoring sister, to stare at the stars through a window facing north.
TWO	Vera decides for the rest of her life, she wants to keep doing this.
FOUR	At school, her physics teacher says that discoveries come from either genius or luck. If they hadn't found it, someone else would have. Marie Curie is his example.

ONE At university,
she calls her thesis
'The Rotation of the Universe'
and is laughed at by a room full of men
twice her age.

THREE At the observatory,
she studies galaxies
when no-one else is interested.

ONE She sees galaxy after galaxy
show her the same
strange
thing.

FOUR She observes an
impossible pattern in nature
over and
over
again.

ONE She publishes.
Twenty one galaxies
showing the impossible.
Twenty one galaxies
staring us in the face,
telling us we know nothing.

FOUR The scientific community try to argue,
but they can't.

THREE Vera Rubin
has found the first
irrefutable evidence
for the existence of
an unknown substance
making up the majority
of the universe's matter.

It is the
smoking gun of
human ignorance.

ONE	A secret that rewrites the universe, arriving with little fanfare, no prize or medal, told to a little girl who stared into the night sky and waited.
FOUR	Waited until the red light from the stars of distant galaxies reached her telescope and told her something no-one had ever known.
ONE	Because a red shift in light means something is moving away from you.
TWO	And if red light is moving away, blue is coming towards you.
THREE	Blue means something is hurtling in your direction at an incomprehensible speed.
FOUR	Blue means nature is gaining on you.
TWO	Blue is an incoming collision.
ONE	Blue is –

*

*We collide with **2026**.*

SUPERVISOR	'We have peered into a new world, and have seen that it is more mysterious

and more complex than we had imagined.
Still more mysteries of the universe remain
hidden.
Their discovery awaits the adventurous
scientists of
the future.'

You quoted Vera Rubin.

You ended your application with
the same sentence as her.
The reason we're all here.

You described the
limitlessness of what
you didn't know.
And then you wrote:

'I like it this way'.

*

GIRLFRIEND *reconnects the microphone and leaves a voice message.*

GIRLFRIEND   Hey Soph,
I got your messages.
All fourteen of them.

I agree.
Time in the dark can be good.
Even a few minutes makes
the light seem so much
more brilliant and clear
when you emerge,
doesn't it?

Maybe the world will look
different than when you left it.
More beautiful.

God, I sound like you.

Anyway,
I hope the unblinding goes well,
if it's the sort of thing that can go well.
I hope you create some new knowledge.

And even if you don't,
I hope you can see what
beautiful things you know already.

*

The PARTICLES *retreat to the curtain, the boundary between realms.*

THREE	Have you worked it out yet?
ONE	The most famous magician of all time.
TWO	The medium who proved herself to science.
THREE	The teacher murdered for her mind.
FOUR	The student unblinding the dark.
ONE	The astronomer who turned the universe inside out.
TWO	Five collisions.
THREE	The same story.
ONE	An invisible majority.
FOUR	Doing the impossible work.

TWO	Invisible, only,

TWO disappears.

THREE	until you look in the right place.

THREE disappears.

*

SOPHIE *and her* SUPERVISOR *one last time.*

SUPERVISOR	Are you ready?
SOPHIE	I don't want it to end.
SUPERVISOR	The experiment?
SOPHIE	All of it.

.

SUPERVISOR	Do you still stay up to stare at the stars, Sophie?
SOPHIE	I think every physicist does.
SUPERVISOR	And how does that make you feel?

.

SOPHIE	Endless.

.

SUPERVISOR	Endless.

A beat has been rising imperceptibly.

It now reaches a height of anticipation.

ONE *and* FOUR *grasp the edges of the blue velvet curtain – the barrier between worlds, and their portal to the unknown.*

They take a last look at the visible universe, at all of us.

And they, too, disappear into the darkness.

The End (?)

APPENDIX

1. Ptolemy's geo-centric model of the universe.

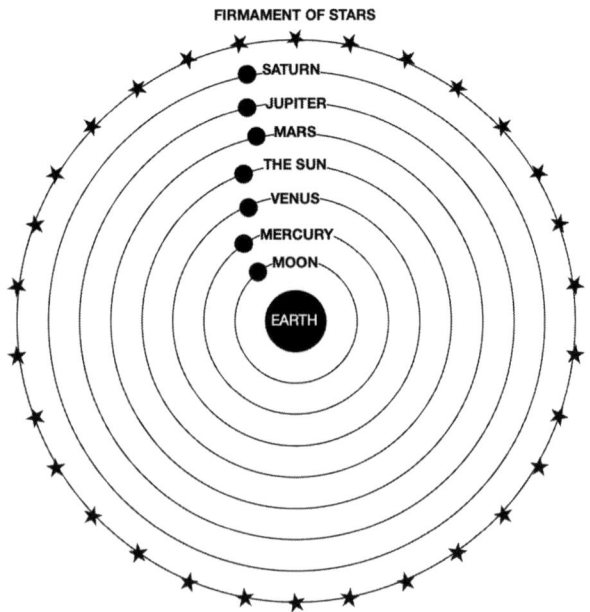

A Nick Hern Book

Aether first published in Great Britain as a paperback original in 2026 by Nick Hern Books Limited, The Glasshouse, 49a Goldhawk Road, London W12 8QP, in association with

Aether copyright © 2026 Emma Howlett

Emma Howlett has asserted her right to be identified as the author of this work

Cover image by Giulia Ferrando

Designed and typeset by Nick Hern Books, London
Printed in Great Britain by Mimeo Ltd, Huntingdon, Cambridgeshire PE29 6XX

A CIP catalogue record for this book is available from the British Library

ISBN 978 1 83904 548 6

CAUTION All rights whatsoever in this play are strictly reserved. Requests to reproduce the text in whole or in part should be addressed to the publisher. This book may not be used, in whole or in part, for the development or training of artificial intelligence technologies or systems.

Amateur Performing Rights Applications for performance, including readings and excerpts, by amateurs in the English language should be addressed to the Performing Rights Department, Nick Hern Books, The Glasshouse, 49a Goldhawk Road, London W12 8QP, *tel* +44 (0)20 8749 4953, *email* rights@nickhernbooks.co.uk, except as follows:

Australia: ORiGiN Theatrical, *email* enquiries@originmusic.com.au, *web* www.origintheatrical.com.au

New Zealand: Play Bureau, 20 Rua Street, Mangapapa, Gisborne, 4010, *tel* +64 21 258 3998, *email* info@playbureau.com

United States and Canada: Independent Talent Group, see details below

Professional Performing Rights Applications for performance by professionals in any medium and in any language throughout the world should be addressed to Independent Talent Group Ltd, 40 Whitfield Street, London W1T 2RH, *tel* +44 (0)20 7636 6565

No performance of any kind may be given unless a licence has been obtained. Applications should be made before rehearsals begin. Publication of this play does not necessarily indicate its availability for performance.

www.nickhernbooks.co.uk/environmental-policy

Nick Hern Books' authorised representative in the EU is
Easy Access System Europe – Mustamäe tee 50, 10621 Tallinn, Estonia
email gpsr.requests@easproject.com

www.nickhernbooks.co.uk

@nickhernbooks